T0407480

What a Copycat!

¡Qué copión!

by Liza Charlesworth

What a Copycat!
¡Qué copión!

by Liza Charlesworth

ISBN: 978-1-338-70351-1
Illustrated by Tammie Lyon
Copyright © 2020 by Liza Charlesworth. All rights reserved.
Published by Scholastic Inc., 557 Broadway, New York, NY 10012

10 9 8 7 6 5 4 3   68   22 23 24 25 26/0

Printed in Jiaxing, China. First printing, June 2020.

Max is a cat.
Jax is a copycat.

Max es un gato.
Jax es un copión.

Max plays with a ball.
Jax plays with a ball, too.
What a copycat!

Max juega con la bola.
Jax también juega con la bola.
¡Qué copión!

Max climbs a tree.
Jax climbs a tree, too.
What a copycat!

Max trepa el árbol.
Jax también trepa el árbol.
¡Qué copión!

Max eats a lot of food.
Jax eats a lot of food, too.
What a copycat!

Max come mucha comida.
Jax también come mucha comida.
¡Qué copión!

Max naps in a chair.
Jax naps in a chair, too.
What a copycat!

Max toma una siesta en el sillón.
Jax también toma
una siesta en el sillón.
¡Qué copión!

Max gets mad.
"Stop being a copycat!"
he says to Jax.

Max se enfada.
—¡Deja de ser un copión!
—le dice a Jax.

Jax says he is sorry.
Max says he is sorry, too.
What a copycat!

Jax dice que lo siente.
Max también dice que lo siente.
¡Qué copión!

English-Spanish
First Little Readers™

ISBN: 978-1-338-70351-1

EAN

9 781338 703511 >

SCHOLASTIC

Robot Land
La Tierra de los Robots

by Liza Charlesworth

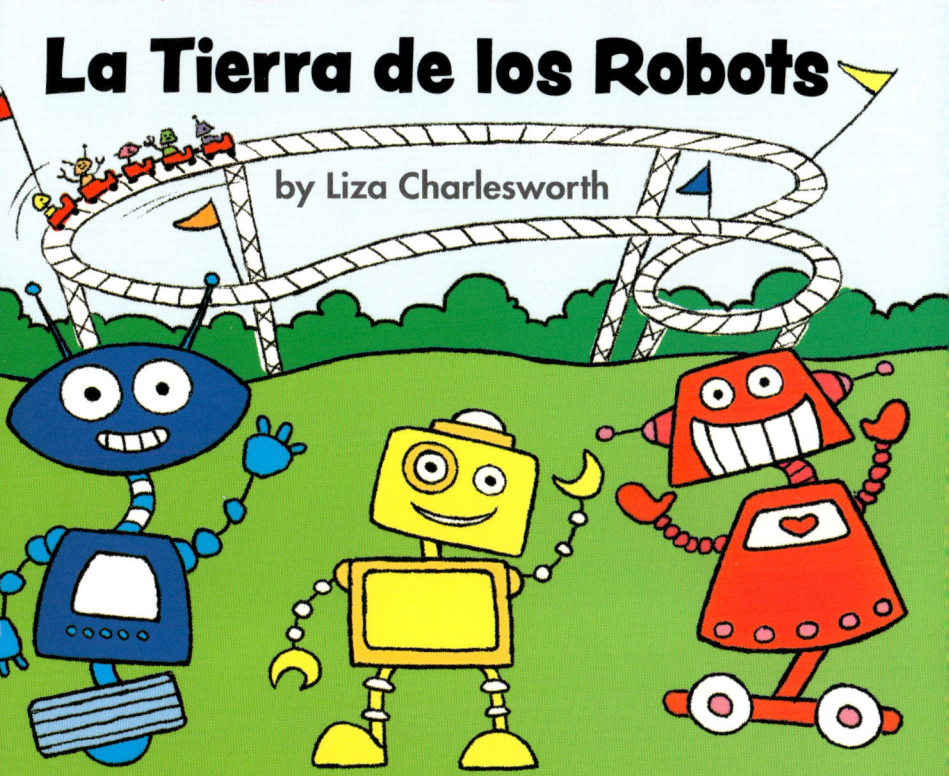

Robot Land
La Tierra de los Robots

by Liza Charlesworth

ISBN: 978-1-338-70349-8
Illustrated by Tammie Lyon
Copyright © 2020 by Liza Charlesworth. All rights reserved.
Published by Scholastic Inc., 557 Broadway, New York, NY 10012

10 9 8 7 6 5 4 3   68   22 23 24 25 26/0

Printed in Jiaxing, China. First printing, June 2020.

Some robots are red.
Some robots are blue.

Algunos robots son rojos.
Otros robots son azules.

Some robots live
in a big robot shoe.

Algunos robots viven
en un gran zapato robot.

Some robots are short.
Some robots are tall.

Algunos robots son bajos.
Otros robots son altos.

Some robots have
a little robot doll.

Algunos robots tienen
muñequitas robot.

Some robots ride.
Some robots jog.
Some robots walk a robot dog.

Algunos robots montan.
Otros robots corren.
Los hay que pasean perros robot.

Some robots love snow.
Some robots love sand.

A algunos robots les encanta la nieve.
A otros robots les encanta la arena.

But all robots
love Robot Land!

¡Pero a todos los robots
les encanta la Tierra de los Robots!

English-Spanish
First Little Readers™

ISBN: 978-1-338-70349-8

EAN

9 781338 703498 >

www.scholastic.com

Can You Hug a Bug?

¿Puedes abrazar a un insecto?

by Liza Charlesworth

Can You Hug a Bug?

¿Puedes abrazar a un insecto?

by Liza Charlesworth

ISBN: 978-1-338-70352-8
Illustrated by Tammie Lyon
Copyright © 2020 by Liza Charlesworth. All rights reserved.
Published by Scholastic Inc., 557 Broadway, New York, NY 10012

10 9 8 7 6 5 4 3   68   22 23 24 25 26/0

Printed in Jiaxing, China. First printing, June 2020.

Can you hug a bug?
Yes! But you have to be very small.

¿Puedes abrazar a un insecto?
¡Sí! Pero tienes que ser
muy pequeño.

Can you hug a giraffe?
Yes! But you have to be very tall.

¿Puedes abrazar a una jirafa?
¡Sí! Pero tienes que ser muy alto.

Can you hug a sloth?
Yes! But you have to be very slow.

¿Puedes abrazar a un oso perezoso?
¡Sí! Pero tienes que ser muy lento.

Can you hug a horse?
Yes! But you have to go, go, go!

¿Puedes abrazar a un caballo?
¡Sí! ¡Pero tienes que salir corriendo!

Can you hug a bird?
Yes! But you have to be in a tree.

¿Puedes abrazar a un pájaro?
¡Sí! Pero tienes que subir a un árbol.

Can you hug a fish?
Yes! But you have to be in the sea.

¿Puedes abrazar a un pez?
¡Sí! Pero tienes que bajar al mar.

Can you hug a monkey?
Yes! But you have to say,
"Eee, eee, eee!"

¿Puedes abrazar a un mono?
¡Sí! Pero tienes que decir:
—¡Uh, uh, ah, ah!

English-Spanish
First Little Readers™

ISBN: 978-1-338-70352-8

EAN

9 781338 703528

SCHOLASTIC

www.scholastic.com

I Am Super!

¡Soy súper!

by Liza Charlesworth

I Am Super!

¡Soy súper!

by Liza Charlesworth

ISBN: 978-1-338-70353-5
Illustrated by Tammie Lyon
Copyright © 2020 by Liza Charlesworth. All rights reserved.
Published by Scholastic Inc., 557 Broadway, New York, NY 10012.

10 9 8 7 6 5 4 3   68   22 23 24 25 26/0

Printed in Jiaxing, China. First printing, June 2020.

Hi!
I am Sam
and I am super!

¡Hola!
Soy Sam
¡y soy súper!

I am super!
I can clean up my room.
Zoom, zoom!

¡Soy súper!
Sé limpiar mi habitación.
¡Zum, zum!

I am super!
I can ride my new bike.
Zoom, zoom!

¡Soy súper!
Sé montar mi bicicleta nueva.
¡Zum, zum!

I am super!
I can eat all my lunch.
Zoom, zoom!

¡Soy súper!
Puedo comerme todo el almuerzo.
¡Zum, zum!

I am super!
I can build a tall tower.
Zoom, zoom!

¡Soy súper!
Sé construir una torre alta.
¡Zum, zum!

I am super!
I can read a big book.
Zoom, zoom!

¡Soy súper!
Sé leer un libro grande.
¡Zum, zum!

I am super!
I can walk my dog.
He is super, too.
Zoom, zoom!

¡Soy súper!
Sé pasear a mi perro.
Él, también, es súper.
¡Zum, zum!

English-Spanish
First Little Readers™

ISBN: 978-1-338-70353-5

EAN

SCHOLASTIC

www.scholastic.com

Scaredy Bat
El murciélago miedoso

by Liza Charlesworth

Scaredy Bat
El murciélago miedoso

by Liza Charlesworth

ISBN: 978-1-338-70354-2
Illustrated by Tammie Lyon
Copyright © 2020 by Liza Charlesworth. All rights reserved.
Published by Scholastic Inc., 557 Broadway, New York, NY 10012

10 9 8 7 6 5 4 3   68   22 23 24 25 26/0

Printed in Jiaxing, China. First printing, June 2020.

This is Pat.
He is a scaredy bat.

Este es Pat.
Es un murciélago miedoso.

Pat saw a black cat.
It was scary.
So he flew away.
Flap, flap!

Pat vio un gato negro.
Daba miedo.
Así que se fue volando.
¡Vuela, vuela!

Pat saw a white ghost.
It was scary.
But he did not fly away.
Why?

Pat vio un fantasma blanco.
Daba miedo.
Pero no pudo irse volando.
¿Por qué?

Because his pal said,
"It is just me. Hee, hee!"

Porque su amigo dijo:
—Soy yo. ¡Ja, ja!

Then Pat and his pal
flew away to play.
Flap, flap!

Entonces, Pat y su amigo
se fueron volando a jugar.
¡Vuela, vuela!

English-Spanish
First Little Readers™

ISBN: 978-1-338-70354-2

EAN

9 781338 703542

SCHOLASTIC

www.scholastic.com

Look at That Princess Go!

Mira a esa princesa en acción!

by Liza Charlesworth

Look at That Princess Go!

¡Mira a esa princesa en acción!

by Liza Charlesworth

ISBN: 978-1-338-70355-9
Illustrated by Tammie Lyon
Copyright © 2020 by Liza Charlesworth. All rights reserved.
Published by Scholastic Inc., 557 Broadway, New York, NY 10012

10 9 8 7 6 5 4 3   68   22 23 24 25 26/0

Printed in Jiaxing, China. First printing, June 2020.

Look at that princess go!
She can run fast.

¡Mira a esa princesa en acción!
Sabe correr rápido.

Look at that princess go!
She can jump high.
She can roll and roll.

¡Mira a esa princesa en acción!
Sabe saltar alto.
Sabe rodar y rodar.

Look at that princess go!
She can ride a horse.

¡Mira a esa princesa en acción!
Sabe montar a caballo.

She can climb in a window.

Sabe subir hasta una ventana.

Look at that princess go!
She can tiptoe.

¡Mira a esa princesa en acción!
Sabe ir de puntillas.

She can swing, too.

También sabe columpiarse.

Look at that princess go!
She can save the day.
Yay!

¡Mira a esa princesa en acción!
Es una heroína.
¡Hurra!

English-Spanish
First Little Readers™

ISBN: 978-1-338-70355-

EAN

9 781338 703559

SCHOLASTIC

www.scholastic.com

Clown Cars
Autos de payasos

by Liza Charlesworth

Clown Cars
Autos de payasos

by Liza Charlesworth

ISBN: 978-1-338-70356-6
Illustrated by Tammie Lyon
Copyright © 2020 by Liza Charlesworth. All rights reserved.
Published by Scholastic Inc., 557 Broadway, New York, NY 10012

10 9 8 7 6 5 4 3   68   22 23 24 25 26/0

Printed in Jiaxing, China. First printing, June 2020.

Look at the big, yellow car!
Who could be inside?

¡Mira ese auto grande y amarillo!
¿Quién irá adentro?

Surprise!
Out comes a big, yellow clown
with a big, yellow flower.

¡Sorpresa!
Es un payaso grande y amarillo,
con una flor grande y amarilla.

Look at the big, orange car!
Who could be inside?

¡Mira ese auto grande y anaranjado
¿Quién irá adentro?

Surprise!
Out comes a big, orange clown
with a big, orange teddy bear.

¡Sorpresa!
Es un payaso grande y anaranjado
con un oso de peluche grande
y anaranjado.

Look at the big, blue car!
Who could be inside?

¡Mira ese auto grande y azul!
¿Quién irá adentro?

Surprise!
Out comes a big, blue clown
with a big, blue cake.

¡Sorpresa!
Es un payaso grande y azul
con un pastel grande y azul.

Yellow, orange, blue!
The clowns have come
to surprise you.

¡Amarillo, anaranjado, azul!
Los payasos vinieron
a darte una sorpresa.

English-Spanish
First Little Readers™

ISBN: 978-1-338-70356-

EAN

9 781338 703566

SCHOLASTIC

www.scholastic.com

Bossy Boots

Las botas mandonas

by Liza Charlesworth

Bossy Boots
Las botas mandonas

by Liza Charlesworth

ISBN: 978-1-338-70357-3
Illustrated by Tammie Lyon
Copyright © 2020 by Liza Charlesworth. All rights reserved.
Published by Scholastic Inc., 557 Broadway, New York, NY 10012

10 9 8 7 6 5 4 3   68   22 23 24 25 26/0

Printed in Jiaxing, China. First printing, June 2020.

One, two!
Meet the bossy boots.

¡Una, dos!
Estas son las botas mandonas.

"Play our game!" they said.
"Okay," said the shoes.

—¡Jueguen en nuestro partido!
—dijeron.
—Está bien —dijeron los zapatos.

3

"Watch our show!" they said.
"Okay," said the shoes.
"Read our book!" they said.
"Okay," said the shoes.

—¡Vean nuestro programa! —dijeron.
—Está bien —dijeron los zapatos.
—¡Lean nuestro libro! —dijeron.
—Está bien —dijeron los zapatos.

But the shoes got mad.
The boots were too bossy!
So they ran away.

Pero los zapatos se enfadaron.
¡Las botas eran demasiado mandonas!
Se fueron corriendo.

"Boo-hoo!" said the bossy boots.
"The shoes will not play with us."

—¡Snif, snif! —dijeron las botas
mandonas—. Los zapatos no quieren
jugar con nosotras.

The boots went to see the shoes.
"Sorry we were so bossy," they said.
"Can we play?"

Las botas fueron a ver a los zapatos.
—Perdonen que fuimos tan mandonas
—dijeron—. ¿Podemos jugar?

"Okay!" said the shoes.
Hooray!

—¡Está bien! —dijeron los zapatos—.
¡Hurra!

English-Spanish
First Little Readers™

ISBN: 978-1-338-70357-

EAN

9 781338 703573 >

SCHOLASTIC

www.scholastic.com

Wiggle, Wiggle
Muévelo, muévelo

by Liza Charlesworth

Wiggle, Wiggle
Muévelo, muévelo

by Liza Charlesworth

ISBN: 978-1-338-70358-0
Illustrated by Tammie Lyon
Copyright © 2020 by Liza Charlesworth. All rights reserved.
Published by Scholastic Inc., 557 Broadway, New York, NY 10012

10 9 8 7 6 5 4 3   68   22 23 24 25 26/0

Printed in Jiaxing, China. First printing, June 2020.

Wiggle, wiggle.
I want my tooth
to fall out.

Muévelo, muévelo.
Quiero que mi diente se caiga.

"Eat an apple," said Mom.
Crunch, crunch, crunch!
But the tooth did not fall out.

—Come una manzana —dice Mamá.
¡Cronch, cronch, cronch!
Pero el diente no se cayó.

"Eat a carrot," said Dad.
Crunch, crunch, crunch!
But the tooth did not fall out.

—Come una zanahoria —dice Papá
¡Cronch, cronch, cronch!
Pero el diente no se cayó.

"Eat a pretzel," said Grandpa.
Crunch, crunch, crunch!
But the tooth did not fall out.

—Come un prétzel —dice Abuelo.
¡Cronch, cronch, cronch!
Pero el diente no se cayó.

"Oh, no!" I said.
"My tooth will never fall out."

—¡Ay, no! —dije—. Mi diente nunca
se va a caer.

Wiggle, wiggle.
Wiggle, wiggle.

Muévelo, muévelo.
Muévelo, muévelo.

Look at me!
Yippee!

Dear Tooth Fairy,
Here is my
tooth!

¡Lo logré!
¡Muy bien!

English-Spanish
First Little Readers™

ISBN: 978-1-338-70358-

SCHOLASTIC

www.scholastic.com

Monster School

Escuela de monstruos

by Liza Charlesworth

Monster School

Escuela de monstruos

by Liza Charlesworth

ISBN: 978-1-338-70359-7
Illustrated by Tammie Lyon
Copyright © 2020 by Liza Charlesworth. All rights reserved.
Published by Scholastic Inc., 557 Broadway, New York, NY 10012

10 9 8 7 6 5 4 3   68   22 23 24 25 26/0

Printed in Jiaxing, China. First printing, June 2020.

What time is it?
It is time for the monsters
to go to school.
They like to see monster friends.

¿Qué hora es?
Es hora de que los monstruos
vayan a la escuela.
Les gusta ver a sus amigos monstruos

What time is it?
It is time for the monsters to read.
They like to read monster books.

¿Qué hora es?
Es hora de que los monstruos lean.
Les gusta leer libros de monstruos.

3

What time is it?
It is time for the monsters to paint.
They like to paint monster pictures.

¿Qué hora es?
Es hora de que los monstruos pinten.
Les gusta pintar dibujos de monstruos.

What time is it?
It is time for the monsters to eat.
They like to eat monster food.

¿Qué hora es?
Es hora de que los monstruos coman.
Les gusta comer comida de monstruos.

5

What time is it?
It is time for the monsters to play.
They like to play monster games.

¿Qué hora es?
Es hora de que los monstruos jueguen
Les gusta jugar juegos de monstruos.

What time is it?
It is time for the monsters to write.
They like to write monster stories.

¿Qué hora es?
Es hora de que los monstruos escriban.
Les gusta escribir cuentos de monstruos.

7

What time is it?
It is time for the monsters
to go home.
They like to ride the monster bus!

¿Qué hora es?
Es hora de que los monstruos
vayan a casa.
¡Les gusta ir en el autobús de monstruos

English-Spanish
First Little Readers™

ISBN: 978-1-338-70359-

EAN

9 781338 703597 >

Mama Dinosaur

Mamá dinosaurio

by Liza Charlesworth

Mama Dinosaur
Mamá dinosaurio

by Liza Charlesworth

ISBN: 978-1-338-70360-3
Illustrated by Tammie Lyon
Copyright © 2020 by Liza Charlesworth. All rights reserved.
Published by Scholastic Inc., 557 Broadway, New York, NY 10012

10 9 8 7 6 5 4 3   68   22 23 24 25 26/0

Printed in Jiaxing, China. First printing, June 2020.

Look!
It is a mama dinosaur.

¡Mira!
Es una mamá dinosaurio.

She can walk.
She can roar.

Puede caminar.
Puede rugir.

She can sleep.
She can snore.

Puede dormir.
Puede roncar.

She can stand up on two feet.

Se puede parar en dos patas.

She can eat and eat and eat!

¡Puede comer y comer y comer!

She can lay eggs in a nest.

Puede poner huevos en un nido.

Crack, crack, crack.
Baby dinos are the best!

Crac, crac, crac.
¡Las crías de dinosaurio son geniales

English-Spanish
First Little Readers™

ISBN: 978-1-338-70360-1

EAN

9 781338 703603

SCHOLASTIC

www.scholastic.com

Pam's Pizza

La pizza de Pam

by Liza Charlesworth

Pam's Pizza
La pizza de Pam

by Liza Charlesworth

ISBN: 978-1-338-70361-0
Illustrated by Tammie Lyon
Copyright © 2020 by Liza Charlesworth. All rights reserved.
Published by Scholastic Inc., 557 Broadway, New York, NY 10012.

10 9 8 7 6 5 4 3   68   22 23 24 25 26/0

Printed in Jiaxing, China. First printing, June 2020.

This is Pam.
She is making a pizza.

Esta es Pam.
Está haciendo una pizza.

2

Pam puts on cheese.
Sprinkle, sprinkle!

Pam pone el queso.
¡Esparce, esparce!

Pam puts on pickles.
She puts on popcorn, too.

Pam pone los pepinillos.
También pone las palomitas de maíz

Pam puts on noodles.
She puts on jam, too.

Pam pone los fideos.
También pone la mermelada.

Pam puts on carrots.
She puts on cookies, too.

Pam pone las zanahorias.
También pone las galletas.

Pam puts the pizza in the oven.
Bake, bake!

Pam pone la pizza en el horno.
¡Hornea, hornea!

Pam's pizza is done!
Do you want some?

¡La pizza de Pam está lista!
¿Quieres un poco?

English-Spanish
First Little Readers™

ISBN: 978-1-338-70361-
EAN
9 781338 703610 >

SCHOLASTIC

www.scholastic.com

Two Little Penguins

Dos pingüinitos

by Liza Charlesworth

Two Little Penguins
Dos pingüinitos

by Liza Charlesworth

ISBN: 978-1-338-70362-7
Illustrated by Tammie Lyon
Copyright © 2020 by Liza Charlesworth. All rights reserved.
Published by Scholastic Inc., 557 Broadway, New York, NY 10012

10 9 8 7 6 5 4 3   68   22 23 24 25 26/0

Printed in Jiaxing, China. First printing, June 2020.

Look!
Two little penguins
hop out of bed.

¡Mira!
Dos pingüinitos
saltan de la cama.

Look!
Two little penguins
ride on a sled.

¡Mira!
Dos pingüinitos
montan en trineo.

Look!
Two little penguins
swim in the sea.

¡Mira!
Dos pingüinitos
nadan en el mar.

Look!
Two little penguins
learn how to ski.

¡Mira!
Dos pingüinitos
aprenden a esquiar.

5

Look!
Two little penguins build a wall.
Two little penguins throw snowballs.

¡Mira!
Dos pingüinitos construyen un muro.
Dos pingüinitos lanzan bolas de nieve.

Look!
Two little penguins
eat ice cream.

¡Mira!
Dos pingüinitos
comen helado.

Shhh!
Two little penguins
lie down to dream.

¡Shhh!
Dos pingüinitos
se acuestan a soñar.

English-Spanish
First Little Readers™

ISBN: 978-1-338-70362

EAN

9 781338 703627

Funny Bunny

El conejito gracioso

by Liza Charlesworth

Funny Bunny
El conejito gracioso

by Liza Charlesworth

ISBN: 978-1-338-70363-4
Illustrated by Tammie Lyon
Copyright © 2020 by Liza Charlesworth. All rights reserved.
Published by Scholastic Inc., 557 Broadway, New York, NY 10012

10 9 8 7 6 5 4 3   68   22 23 24 25 26/0

Printed in Jiaxing, China. First printing, June 2020.

Meet a cute bunny.
He is so funny!

Este es un conejito lindo.
¡Es muy gracioso!

He makes a silly face.
That bunny is so funny!

Hace muecas.
¡Ese conejito es muy gracioso!

He sings a silly song.
That bunny is so funny!

Canta una canción chistosa.
¡Ese conejito es muy gracioso!

He puts on silly glasses.
That bunny is so funny!

Se pone gafas chistosas.
¡Ese conejito es muy gracioso!

He does a silly dance.
Hop, hop, hop. Boppity, bop.
That bunny is so funny!

Hace un baile chistoso.
¡Salta, salta, salta!
¡Salta un poco más!
¡Ese conejito es muy gracioso!

He buys carrots.
Hey, that is not funny.

Compra zanahorias.
¡Un momento! Eso no es gracioso.

Oh, yes it is.
That bunny is so funny!

¡Ah, sí lo es!
¡Ese conejito es muy gracioso!

English-Spanish
First Little Readers™

ISBN: 978-1-338-70363

EAN

9 781338 703634

SCHOLASTIC

www.scholastic.com

Shark and Crab

Tiburón y Cangrejo

by Liza Charlesworth

Shark and Crab

Tiburón y Cangrejo

by Liza Charlesworth

ISBN: 978-1-338-70350-4
Illustrated by Tammie Lyon
Copyright © 2020 by Liza Charlesworth. All rights reserved.
Published by Scholastic Inc., 557 Broadway, New York, NY 10012

10 9 8 7 6 5 4 3   68   22 23 24 25 26/0

Printed in Jiaxing, China. First printing, June 2020.

Ready, set, go!
Shark and Crab had a race.

¡Preparados, listos, fuera!
Tiburón y Cangrejo corrieron
una carrera.

Shark went fast.
Swim, swim, swim.

Tiburón iba rápido.
Nada, nada, nada.

Crab went slow.
Crawl, crawl, crawl.

Cangrejo iba despacio.
Camina, camina, camina.

What did Shark do?
He took a nap.
Snore, snore, snore.

¿Qué hizo Tiburón?
Tomó una siesta.
Ronca, ronca, ronca.

What did Crab do?
She did not stop.
Crawl, crawl, crawl.

¿Qué hizo Cangrejo?
No paró.
Camina, camina, camina.

Shark woke up.
Oh, no!
Swim, swim, swim.

Tiburón despertó.
¡Ay, no!
Nada, nada, nada.

But Shark was too late.
Crab won the race.
Way to go, Crab!

Pero Tiburón llegó muy tarde.
Cangrejo ganó la carrera.
¡Así se hace, Cangrejo!

English-Spanish
First Little Readers™

ISBN: 978-1-338-70350

EAN

9 781338 703504 >

The Missing Twin

El gemelo perdido

by Liza Charlesworth

The Missing Twin
El gemelo perdido

by Liza Charlesworth

ISBN: 978-1-338-70364-1
Illustrated by Tammie Lyon
Copyright © 2020 by Liza Charlesworth. All rights reserved.
Published by Scholastic Inc., 557 Broadway, New York, NY 10012

10 9 8 7 6 5 4 3   68   22 23 24 25 26/0

Printed in Jiaxing, China. First printing, June 2020.

"Oh, no!" said Little Sock.
I lost my twin.

—¡Ay, no! —dijo Calcetín—.
Perdí a mi gemelo.

He looked in the basket.
But he only saw Pants.
Where was his twin?

Buscó en la canasta.
Pero allí solo vio a Pantalones.
¿Dónde estaba su gemelo?

He looked in the closet.
But he only saw Coat.
Where was his twin?

Buscó en el armario.
Pero allí solo vio a Abrigo.
¿Dónde estaba su gemelo?

He looked on the shelf.
But he only saw Sweater.
Where was his twin?

Buscó en el estante.
Pero allí solo vio a Suéter.
¿Dónde estaba su gemelo?

He looked in the drawer.
But he only saw Underwear.
Where was his twin?

Buscó en el cajón.
Pero allí solo vio a Calzoncillo.
¿Dónde estaba su gemelo?

He looked in the washer.
Guess what he saw?
His twin!

Buscó en la lavadora.
¿Adivina a quién vio?
¡A su gemelo!

So Little Sock
jumped in.
Time for a swim!

Así que Calcetín
saltó adentro.
¡Es hora de nadar!

English-Spanish
First Little Readers™

MSCHOLASTIC

www.scholastic.com

ISBN: 978-1-338-7036

EAN

9 781338 703641

The Hot Dog

El perrito caliente

by Liza Charlesworth

The Hot Dog

El perrito caliente

by Liza Charlesworth

ISBN: 978-1-338-70365-8
Illustrated by Tammie Lyon
Copyright © 2020 by Liza Charlesworth. All rights reserved.
Published by Scholastic Inc., 557 Broadway, New York, NY 10012

10 9 8 7 6 5 4 3   68   22 23 24 25 26/0

Printed in Jiaxing, China. First printing, June 2020.

This is **Bob**.
He is a dog.

Este es Bob.
Bob es un perro.

Bob runs on the beach.
The beach is hot.
So he is a hot dog!

Bob corre en la playa.
En la playa hace calor.
¡Así que él es un perrito caliente!

Bob rolls in the sand.
The sand is hot.
So he is a hot dog!

Bob rueda sobre la arena.
La arena está caliente.
¡Así que él es un perrito caliente!

Bob sits in the chair.
The chair is hot.
So he is a hot dog!

Bob se sienta en la tumbona.
La tumbona está caliente.
¡Así que él es un perrito caliente!

Bob lies on the towel.
The towel is hot.
So he is a hot dog!

Bob se echa en la toalla.
La toalla está caliente.
¡Así que es un perrito caliente!

Bob jumps in the water.
SPLASH!

Bob salta al agua.
¡Chof!

The water is cold.
So Bob is now a cold dog.
Brrrrr!

El agua está fría.
Así que Bob es ahora un perrito frío.
¡Brrr!

English-Spanish
First Little Readers™

ISBN: 978-1-338-70365-

EAN

9 781338 703658

www.scholastic.com

Cranky Kitty
El gatito malhumorado

by Liza Charlesworth

Cranky Kitty
El gatito malhumorado

by Liza Charlesworth

ISBN: 978-1-338-70366-5
Illustrated by Tammie Lyon
Copyright © 2020 by Liza Charlesworth. All rights reserved.
Published by Scholastic Inc., 557 Broadway, New York, NY 10012

10 9 8 7 6 5 4 3   68   22 23 24 25 26/0

Printed in Jiaxing, China. First printing, June 2020.

Guess what?
This kitty is cranky!

¿Sabes qué?
¡Este gatito está de mal humor!

She will not eat.
This kitty is cranky!

No quiere comer.
¡Este gatito está de mal humor!

She will not play.
This kitty is cranky!

No quiere jugar.
¡Este gatito está de mal humor!

She will not say, "Meow."
This kitty is cranky!

No quiere decir: "Miau".
¡Este gatito está de mal humor!

What WILL this cranky kitty do?
She will take a nap.
Zzzzzzz!

¿Qué QUIERE hacer este gatito?
Quiere tomar una siesta.
¡Zzzzz!

Wake up, cranky kitty!

¡Despierta, gatito malhumorado!

Guess what?
Cranky kitty had a great nap.
Now she is a happy cat!

Prrrrrr.

¿Sabes qué?
El gatito malhumorado tomó
una buena siesta.
¡Ahora es un gatito feliz!

English-Spanish
First Little Readers™

ISBN: 978-1-338-70366-5

EAN

9 781338 703665 >

SCHOLASTIC

www.scholastic.com

Hippo's Hiccups

Hipopótamo con hipo

by Liza Charlesworth

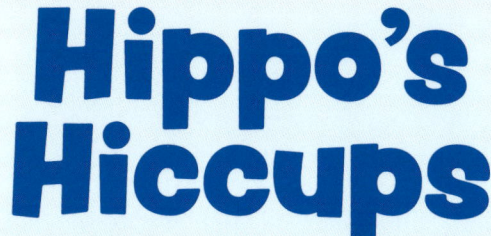

Hiccup!

Hippo's Hiccups

Hipopótamo con hipo

by Liza Charlesworth

ISBN: 978-1-338-70348-1
Illustrated by Tammie Lyon
Copyright © 2020 by Liza Charlesworth. All rights reserved.
Published by Scholastic Inc., 557 Broadway, New York, NY 10012
10 9 8 7 6 5 4 3   68   22 23 24 25 26/0
Printed in Jiaxing, China. First printing, June 2020.

"Hiccup!" said Hippo.
Hippo had the hiccups.
His friends came to help.

—¡Hipo! —dijo Hipopótamo.
Hipopótamo tenía hipo.
Sus amigos vinieron a ayudar.

"Drink water," said Giraffe.
But that did not work.
"Hiccup!" said Hippo.

—Bebe agua —dijo Jirafa.
Pero eso no funcionó.
—¡Hipo! —dijo Hipopótamo.

"Spin around," said Zebra.
But that did not work.
"Hiccup!" said Hippo.

—Da vueltas —dijo Cebra.
Pero eso no funcionó.
—¡Hipo! —dijo Hipopótamo.

"Stand on your head," said Monkey.
But that did not work.
"Hiccup!" said Hippo.

—Párate de cabeza —dijo Mono.
Pero eso no funcionó.
—¡Hipo! —dijo Hipopótamo.

5

"ROAR!" said Lion.
That DID work.

—¡GROOOAR! —dijo León.
Eso sí funcionó.

Lion scared Hippo.
So no more hiccups!

León asustó a Hipopótamo.
No hubo más hipo.

"Thank you," said Hippo.
"Now can you help me
to stop shaking?"

—Gracias —dijo Hipopótamo—.
Ahora, ¿me puedes ayudar
a dejar de temblar?

English-Spanish
First Little Readers™

ISBN: 978-1-338-70348-

EAN

9 781338 703481

■SCHOLASTIC

www.scholastic.com

Birthday Bear

El cumpleañero

by Liza Charlesworth

Birthday Bear

El cumpleañero

by Liza Charlesworth

ISBN: 978-1-338-70367-2
Illustrated by Tammie Lyon
Copyright © 2020 by Liza Charlesworth. All rights reserved.
Published by Scholastic Inc., 557 Broadway, New York, NY 10012

10 9 8 7 6 5 4 3   68   22 23 24 25 26/0

Printed in Jiaxing, China. First printing, June 2020.

"It is my birthday!" said Ben.
"I am five."

—Hoy es mi cumpleaños —dijo
Ben—. ¡Cumplo cinco años!

"Happy birthday!" said Papa.
"Here are five apples."

—¡Feliz cumpleaños! —dijo
Papá—. Aquí tienes cinco manzanas.

"Happy birthday!" said Mama.
"Here are five bananas."

—¡Feliz cumpleaños! —dijo
Mamá—. Aquí tienes cinco plátanos.

"Happy birthday!" said Brother.
"Here are five oranges."

—¡Feliz cumpleaños! —dijo
Hermano—. Aquí tienes cinco naranjas.

"Happy birthday!" said Sister.
"Here are five pears."

—¡Feliz cumpleaños! —dijo
Hermana—. Aquí tienes cinco peras.

"Thank you," said Ben.
"I know what to do."

—Gracias —dijo Ben—.
Ya sé qué hacer.

Ben made fruit salad to share.
What a nice bear!

Happy Birthday!

Ben hizo una ensalada
de frutas para compartir.
¡Qué buen oso!

English-Spanish
First Little Readers™

ISBN: 978-1-338-70367-

EAN

9 781338 703672

SCHOLASTIC

www.scholastic.com

Dog Tricks

Trucos de perro

by Liza Charlesworth

Dog Tricks
Trucos de perro

by Liza Charlesworth

ISBN: 978-1-338-70370-2
Illustrated by Tammie Lyon
Copyright © 2020 by Liza Charlesworth. All rights reserved.
Published by Scholastic Inc., 557 Broadway, New York, NY 10012

10 9 8 7 6 5 4 3   68   22 23 24 25 26/0

Printed in Jiaxing, China. First printing, June 2020.

This is my dog, Nick.
He can do lots of tricks.

Este es mi perro, Nick.
Sabe hacer muchos trucos.

Nick can sit.
Nick can jump.

Nick sabe sentarse.
Nick sabe saltar.

Nick can swing.
Up, up, up!

Nick sabe columpiarse,
¡muy, muy alto!

Nick can ride a bike
all by himself!

Nick sabe montar en bicicleta,
¡sin ayuda!

Nick can tap on a hat.
Tap, tap, tap!

Nick sabe darle unos golpecitos
a un sombrero.
¡Tic, tic, tic!

Out comes a furry cat.
Wow!

Saca un gato peludo.
¡Guau!

Now I have a dog
and a cat.

Ahora tengo un perro
y un gato.

English-Spanish
First Little Readers™

ISBN: 978-1-338-70370-2

EAN

9 781338 703702

SCHOLASTIC

www.scholastic.com

Little Bird's Surprise
La sorpresa de Pajarito

by Liza Charlesworth

Little Bird's Surprise
La sorpresa de Pajarito

by Liza Charlesworth

ISBN: 978-1-338-70371-9
Illustrated by Tammie Lyon
Copyright © 2020 by Liza Charlesworth. All rights reserved.
Published by Scholastic Inc., 557 Broadway, New York, NY 10012

10 9 8 7 6 5 4 3   68   22 23 24 25 26/0

Printed in Jiaxing, China. First printing, June 2020.

Bump, clunk!
Little Bird fell out
of the nest.

Golpe, ¡pum!
Pajarito se cayó
del nido.

The nest was up so high!
How would he ever get back home?

¡El nido estaba muy alto!
¿Cómo regresaría a casa?

"I know," said Little Bird.
"I will jump up to the nest."
Jump, jump, jump!
But that did not work.

—¡Ya sé! —dijo Pajarito—.
Saltaré hasta el nido.
¡Salta, salta, salta!
Pero eso no funcionó.

"I know," said Little Bird.
"I will climb up to the nest."
Climb, climb, climb!
But that did not work.

—¡Ya sé! —dijo Pajarito—.
Treparé hasta el nido.
¡Trepa, trepa, trepa!
Pero eso no funcionó.

Little Bird began to cry.
He flapped his wings
to dry his tears.

Pajarito comenzó a llorar.
Batió sus alas para
secar sus lágrimas.

Flap, flap, flap!
What a surprise!
Little Bird could fly.

¡Bate, bate, bate!
¡Qué sorpresa!
Pajarito podía volar.

Little Bird flew up to the nest.
"Welcome home," said Mom.
"You are just in time for dinner!"

Pajarito voló hasta el nido.
—Bienvenido a casa —dijo Mamá—,
¡llegaste a tiempo para la cena!

English-Spanish
First Little Readers™

ISBN: 978-1-338-70371-9

EAN

9 781338 703719

SCHOLASTIC

www.scholastic.com

Hermit Crab's Home

a casa del cangrejo ermitaño

by Liza Charlesworth

Hermit Crab's Home

La casa del cangrejo ermitaño

by Liza Charlesworth

ISBN: 978-1-338-70372-6
Illustrated by Tammie Lyon
Copyright © 2020 by Liza Charlesworth. All rights reserved.
Published by Scholastic Inc., 557 Broadway, New York, NY 10012

10 9 8 7 6 5 4 3   68   22 23 24 25 26/0

Printed in Jiaxing, China. First printing, June 2020.

This is a hermit crab.
He needs a home.

Este es un cangrejo ermitaño.
Necesita una casa.

He sees a castle.
Could it be a home?
No, it is too big.

Ve un castillo.
¿Podría ser una casa?
No, es demasiado grande.

He sees a bottle.
Could it be a home?
No, it is too small.

Ve una botella.
¿Podría ser una casa?
No, es demasiado pequeña.

He sees a shoe.
Could it be a home?
No, it is too stinky.

Ve un zapato.
¿Podría ser una casa?
No, es demasiado apestoso.

He sees a blanket.
Could it be a home?
No, it is too crowded.

Ve una toalla de playa.
¿Podría ser una casa?
No, está demasiado llena de gente.

He sees a shell.
Could it be a home?
Yes, it is not too big or small
or stinky or crowded.

Ve una concha de mar.
¿Podría ser una casa?
Sí, no es demasiado grande,
ni demasiado pequeña,
ni demasiado apestosa,
ni tiene demasiada gente.

It is just right!
Good night.

¡Es perfecta!
Buenas noches.

English-Spanish
First Little Readers™

ISBN: 978-1-338-70372-6

EAN

9 781338 703726 >

Jay's Big Day
El gran día de Jay

by Liza Charlesworth

Jay's Big Day
El gran día de Jay

by Liza Charlesworth

ISBN: 978-1-338-70373-3
Illustrated by Tammie Lyon
Copyright © 2020 by Liza Charlesworth. All rights reserved.
Published by Scholastic Inc., 557 Broadway, New York, NY 10012

10 9 8 7 6 5 4 3   68   22 23 24 25 26/0

Printed in Jiaxing, China. First printing, June 2020.

"Today is a big day!" said Jay.

—¡Hoy es un gran día! —dijo Jay.

"I will play soccer," he said.
Run, run, run!

—Jugaré al fútbol —dijo.
¡Corre, corre, corre!

"Then I will swim," he said.
Splash, splash, splash!

—Entonces, iré a nadar —dijo.
¡Salpica, salpica, salpica!

"Then I will ride my bike," he said.
Go, go, go!

—Entonces, montaré en bicicleta —dijo.
¡Vamos, vamos, vamos!

"Then I will do karate," he said.
Kick, kick, kick!

—Entonces, practicaré karate —dijo.
¡Patea, patea, patea!

"Then I will dance," he said.
Spin, spin, spin!

—Entonces, bailaré —dijo.
¡Vueltas, vueltas, vueltas!

What did Jay say next?
Nothing! He fell asleep.
Shh, shh, shh!

¿Qué dijo Jay después?
¡Nada!, se quedó dormido.
¡Shhh, shhh, shhh!

English-Spanish
First Little Readers™

SCHOLASTIC

www.scholastic.com

ISBN: 978-1-338-70373-3

EAN

9 781338 703733 >

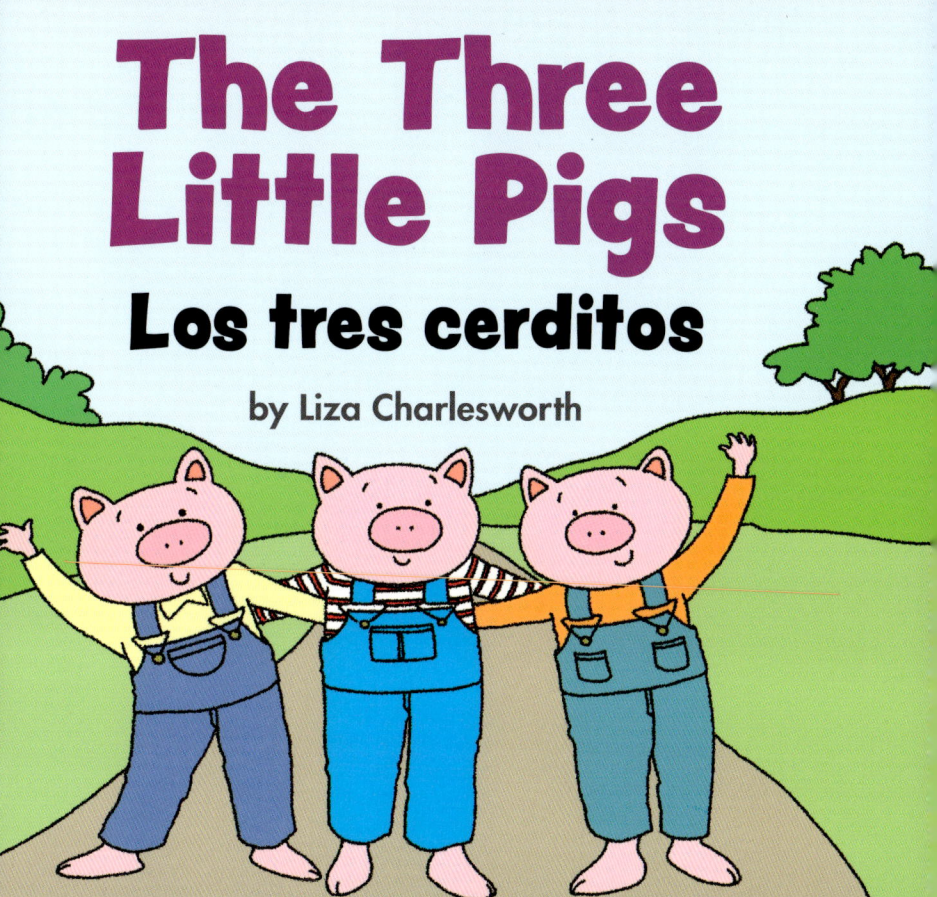

The Three Little Pigs

Los tres cerditos

by Liza Charlesworth

The Three Little Pigs

Los tres cerditos

by Liza Charlesworth

ISBN: 978-1-338-70374-0
Illustrated by Tammie Lyon
Copyright © 2020 by Liza Charlesworth. All rights reserved.
Published by Scholastic Inc., 557 Broadway, New York, NY 10012.

10 9 8 7 6 5 4 3   68   22 23 24 25 26/0

Printed in Jiaxing, China. First printing, June 2020.

See the three little pigs.
See the big wolf.

Mira los tres cerditos.
Mira el lobo grande.

This pig made a house of hay.
Huff and puff!
The wolf blew it down.

Este cerdo hizo una casa de paja.
¡Sopla y sopla!
El lobo la derribó.

This pig made a house of sticks.
Huff and puff!
The wolf blew it down.

Este cerdo hizo una casa de palos.
¡Sopla y sopla!
El lobo la derribó.

This pig made a house of bricks.
Huff and puff!

Este cerdo hizo una casa de ladrillos.
¡Sopla y sopla!

Huff and puff!
Huff and puff!
Huff and puff!

¡Sopla y sopla!
¡Sopla y sopla!
¡Sopla y sopla!

The wolf could not
blow it down.
So he ran away.

El lobo no pudo derribarla,
así que se fue corriendo.

Happy dance!

¡A bailar!

English-Spanish
First Little Readers™

ISBN: 978-1-338-70374-0

EAN

9 781338 703740 >

www.scholastic.com